THE GREAT AMERICAN MOON PIE® HANDBOOK

By RON DICKSON

(With help from William M. Clark and others who wish to remain anonymous)

Cartoons by SCRAWLS

Peachtree Publishers, Ltd.

Published by
PEACHTREE PUBLISHERS, LTD.
494 Armour Circle, N.E.
Atlanta, Georgia 30324

Manufactured in the United States of America

First printing

Library of Congress Catalog Number 85-60339

ISBN: 0-931948-67-3

Dedication

To Janet, whose cheerful encouragement made this project a delightful experience.

Sam C. Rawls

To Patricia, who inspired me with some of the greatest ideas in the Handbook.

William M. Clark

To Elizabeth, Jean, John, Lynda, and Elisabeth who, for several years, supported my dedication to the Handbook and the Noble Cause.

Ronald W. Dickson

Disclaimer

All statements of fact in this book are either accurate or otherwise.

Acknowledgements

The entire staff of the Chattanooga Bakery, Inc., has been most helpful and encouraging with the creation of the Handbook. Special thanks are due:

Sam Campbell, III, President, who permitted us to contact his staff for information.

John Kosik, Executive Vice President, who provided history of the Moon Pie and encouraged and advised us on many things.

Sam Campbell, IV, Sales Manager, whose friendly support and information kept the project moving.

F. A. Bishop, Manager of Distribution, who promptly shipped Moon Pies to us and shared some of the folklore he had acquired over many years.

Bill Jones, who helped us obtain first quality T-shirts, hats, and jackets.

Geneva Smith, Executive Secretary, who cheerfully helped coordinate conversations with the staff.

And finally, Bill Clark, previously of New York State, became an enthusiastic contributor with several clever and profound stories. Needing a sense of direction and noble purpose in his life, he also became the first editor of the Handbook. He rescued many ideas expressed in a crude manner and rewrote them in a polished form. His enthusiasm kept the project moving ahead.

Table of Contents

Preface

The Great American Moon Pie Handbook had its humble beginnings in Charlotte, North Carolina, in the offices of a large international corporation. To many of the native employees, it quickly became obvious that the workers and managers imported from some culturally backward regions of this country were totally ignorant of Southern culture, gentle humor, and the Moon Pie. In a spirit of hospitality and sly amusement, the natives began teaching the newcomers the history, folklore, culture, honorable traditions, and etiquette regarding the Noble Snack. When facts were missing, wild imagination and creativity took over.

Having no culture of their own of which to be proud, the grateful newcomers eagerly learned the Moon Pie Manners and how to enjoy snacking with cultured and refined people. These newly acquired social skills enabled them to be quickly accepted by their new friends and neighbors.

A booklet of about a dozen pages was written to help spread the good news as more foreigners came to work. The booklet began to grow; many employees devoted their entire lunch hour, often the most creative part of the day, to adding new material to the book. Their brilliance and wit were astounding and occasionally bordered on the profound. When word of the Handbook leaked out through the local press, the demand for copies became overwhelming. It was obvious that publication was required.

The Moon Pie Cultural Club, with World Headquarters in Charlotte, had been created to spread the story of the Moon Pie and to establish Club chapters throughout the civilized world. So its devoted Executive Director, Ron Dickson, set out to find a bold and creative publisher who would make the Handbook available to cultured and refined people everywhere.

In November of 1983, the Director sent a copy of the Handbook to Sam C. Rawls, the gifted cartoonist who illustrated the book *How to Speak Southern*. Mr. Rawls, deeply moved by the Handbook and inspired by a second great opportunity to bring more culture to America, drew about twenty cartoons over the Thanksgiving holidays. He sent them to World Headquarters of the Club and, in his typically humble way, suggested that the cartoons be used instead of photographs in the Handbook.

A partnership was formed and the intensive search for the right publisher began. Dozens of rejections were received from publishers located in the Snow Belt. It seemed that most of them had lost their sense of humor and, having no real culture of their own, could not appreciate the noble traditions of others.

Refusing to admit defeat, Sam and Ron noted that the "ring eclipse" of May 30, 1984, resembled a chocolate Moon Pie with the marshmallow oozing out all around the Pie. The shadow of the eclipse passed over Columbus, Georgia, (home of R.C. Cola), Atlanta (home of Sam and Coca-Cola), near Chattanooga, Tennessee, (home of the Moon Pie), and over Charlotte (home of Ron and The Moon Pie Cultural Club), and then out over the Atlantic Ocean. It completely bypassed the Snow Belt publishers. Millions of people wondered how the path of the eclipse had been arranged to pass over such significant locations. Furthermore, it all happened on Sam's birthday.

Believing this to be a sign from the heavens, Sam and Ron concentrated their search for a publisher located only in the path of the eclipse. Consequently, the manuscript was sent to Peachtree Publishers, Ltd., in Atlanta, who decided on October 18, 1984, to print the Handbook and make it available throughout the civilized world. In the history of America, this date is second in importance only to that Great Day on which the first Moon Pie was created, whatever that day was.

In The Beginning . . .

THE MAN AMBLED through the door of the Chattanooga Bakery looking tired and hungry. Life on the road as a traveling salesman was not easy in 1919. He set down his bag of samples and order forms, beat his dusty hat against the side of his leg, and walked longingly toward the display cases filled to overflowing with cookies and cakes.

"Could I hep ya?" asked the young clerk.

The salesman walked up and down the long counter, searching for precisely the right item that would satisfy his discriminating taste buds. "Well," said the stranger, "I been on the road for two months now, and I been looking forward to this stop. Shoot fire, I been dreaming about it. But I be honest with ya — what I got a hankering for, you ain't got."

"Gosh, sir," said the perplexed clerk, "we got more'n two hunnerd kinds of cookies and cakes here. Seems like one of 'em oughta do you."

"No, I just don't see it," he said, shaking his head and burrowing his free hand deeper into his pocket. "What I got in mind is a couple of soft cookies with a little marshmallow 'tween 'em and chocolate all over it. But I 'spect a fellow'd have to go plumb to the moon to find a pie like that. Danged if I don't think it'd sell, though."

The name of that traveling visionary has been lost to the ages, but his idea lives as a testimonial to truth, justice, and the American way. Within weeks of his suggestion, the Chattanooga Bakery produced the first Moon Pie and the world was changed forevermore. In the three score and six years since the Moon Pie was brought forth upon this land, people of good breeding and strong appetite have been nurtured by this heavenly delight and people of depraved cultures (usually places covered with snow and ice) have been asking, "Jeez, guys, what da heck's a Moon Pie?"

Connoisseurs of this noble snack take great pride in answering that question. A Moon Pie consists of two cookies, each about four inches in diameter and reminiscent of graham crackers, although the exact recipe is a closely guarded secret. Between the two cookies is a layer of marshmallow approximately one-fourth inch thick. Depending upon the flavor to be created, the sandwich is drenched with a generous coating of chocolate, vanilla, banana, or coconut flavored frosting. The result is a delicious pastry with just enough moisture to make a wonderful snack food. If it tasted any better, it probably would be illegal.

Moon Pie sandwiches are wrapped in clear cellophane so that the colors (which distinguish the flavors) show through; the banana Moon Pie is a pale, delicate yellow color; vanilla is a creamy white; chocolate is dark brown; and coconut is off-white. Consequently, even illiterate customers can be assured of getting the Moon Pie of their choice. It's sort of like Garanimals for the palate. Color blind customers should seek assistance from sympathetic clerks.

The original Moon Pie was approximately four and one-half

14

inches in diameter and sold for a nickel. Later the size was reduced to the present four inches in diameter to accommodate vending machines. In 1969, marketing history was made again when the Chattanooga Bakery introduced the Double Decker Moon Pie, featuring two layers of marshmallow and three delectable cookies. The Double Decker is available through finer grocery and convenience stores.

Moon Pies are sold individually and in boxes of twelve. Cases of twelve boxes (twelve dozen) also are available upon request. Double Deckers are sold individually, in boxes of twelve, and in cases of six dozen. Cartons of thirty or fifty Pies, loosely packed, are sold to vending machine operators.

Although no total sales figures have been kept since the conception in 1919, the bakery today produces as many as 300,000 Moon Pies per day. And the popularity of the Noble Snack is not limited to the more knowledgeable regions of the United States. The Chattanooga Bakery now has a licensing agreement with the Tohato Baking Company of Japan to produce "Massi Pies." *Massi* means marshmallow in Japanese and is used instead of "Moon," since the word *moon* is sacred in Japan.

The success of the original marshmallow sandwich has attracted numerous imitators, but none can use the name "Moon Pie" since it is registered. Instead, references to their products must use their own registered name or the term *marshmallow sandwich*. While it would be discourteous to mention names, it should be noted that one of the imitators has achieved incredible success in duplicating exactly the flavor and texture of cardboard; another has imitated perfectly the texture and aroma of sawdust; and yet another has matched the texture of glue.

These pretenders, miffed by their inability to unseat the King, have conducted campaigns of rumor and innuendo against Moon Pies for years. They have scurrilously suggested that some Faustian deal lurks behind the success of Moon Pies.

Such charges flourished recently when Moon Pie aficionado D. W. Smart, who has done extensive research into the origin of the Noble Snack, jolted the academic world by publishing his "E.T. Theory" in the *National Enquirer*. Smart suggested that the mysterious traveling salesman who made his historic visit to the Chattanooga Bakery on that fateful day in 1919 was, in reality, an extraterrestrial blessed with intelligence and culture far in advance of our own. His gift to our civilization, Smart proposed, was the Moon Pie.

"The name *Moon* Pie was no coincidence at all," wrote Smart, "but rather a clue left for future generations. If my theory isn't so, then just explain to me why Rod Serling died while working on a television documentary entitled, 'Snack Foods of the Gods.'"

Smart's theory that extraterrestrials brought Moon Pies to earth could explain some quotes by famous people that have perplexed historians for years. In fact, many of these original quotes were modified because historians couldn't figure out their meanings.

For example, it is recorded in faded documents that Richard III of England actually said, "My kingdom for a Moon Pie!," but Samuel Johnson later inserted a horse into the quote because he couldn't find "Moon Pie" in his dictionary.

Nathan Hale, that great American patriot, obviously was thinking about the starving soldiers when he uttered those famous last words, "I regret that I have but one Moon Pie to give for my country." You see, Moon Pies were not packaged and sold by the dozen until midway through the twentieth century.

THE ONLY THING WE HAVE TO FEAR... IS RUNNING OUT OF MOON PIES...

"The only thing we have to fear is . . . running out of Moon Pies," was the challenge which Franklin D. Roosevelt gave to America during the Great Depression. He knew full well that our productivity depended on a supply of Moon Pies on the farms, in the factories, and in the offices of the nation.

"Let them eat Moon Pies . . ." was spoken in an icy voice by Marie Antoinette of France in disdainful regard to the starving peasants.

"I shall return . . . for a Moon Pie." That was the only reason General Douglas MacArthur would return to the Philippines in World War II.

"Give me Moon Pies or give me death!" was the original battle cry of Patrick Henry during the American Revolution.

Moon Pie Slogans

HISTORY IS NOT the only place, however, where quotations about Moon Pies have been plagiarized. Madison Avenue advertising executives also have pilfered from the warehouse of Moon Pie endorsements. Following are some sayings which originally applied to Moon Pies but later became popular with other products:

"I'd walk a mile for a Moon Pie."

"A Moon Pie a day keeps the doctor away."

"Love is never having to say, 'Honey, we're out of Moon Pies.'"

"Moon Pie — A little dab'll never do you."

"I'd rather fight than switch from Moon Pies."

"Baseball, hot dogs, Moon Pies, and Chevrolet."

"Bet you can't eat just one . . . Moon Pie."

"America is bullish on Moon Pies."

23

"We will sell no Moon Pie after its time." (Although it should be noted that the Moon Pie has an unusually long shelf life — approximately sixty days.)

"Moon Pies are good to the last bite."

"Moon Pies taste good like a marshmallow sandwich should."

Sing Along With A Moon Pie

THE MOON PIE ALSO has been immortalized in song, although the original lyrics, in many cases, were changed. Following are several popular songs from the past with their intended lyrics:

Chattanooga Moon Pie
(Sung to the tune of "Chattanooga Choo-Choo")

Pardon me, boy, is that a Chattanooga Moon Pie?
The best in the land, gee, it looks grand!

This ain't a ploy, I'd love a Chattanooga Moon Pie.
Fresh from the box, I'd trade you my socks.

I remember bein' just a tyke upon my Daddy's knee,
A Moon Pie stuffed into my mouth along with R.C.

Dinner in the diner couldn't have been finer,
Thanks to the chef who served Moon Pie fricassee.

Pardon me, boy, is that a Chattanooga Moon Pie?
Oh, it smells divine, I wish it were mine.

Now don't get annoyed, I need a Chattanooga Moon Pie.
Marshmallow inside, a taste you can't hide.

Ballad of the Unknown Salesman
(Sung to the tune of "Battle of New Orleans")

In 1919 he took that fateful trip
To the Chattanooga Bakery
With a handy little tip.

"Ya take two cookies
And ya coat 'em up with goo,
Put a mallow in the middle
And ya might sell one or two."

Chorus: We made them Pies and the orders started comin',
        Nearly twice as many as there was a while ago.
        Made some more and they began a'sellin',
        From north of Mississippi to the Gulf of Mexico.

He left that day never to return,
Though they tried a hundred times
His name they never learned.

His pies will live forever
And of this I am sure,
His place will be remembered
In the halls of Moon Pie lore!

Chorus: We made them Pies and the orders started comin',
        Nearly twice as many as there was a while ago.
        Made some more and they began a'sellin',
        From north of Mississippi to the Gulf of Mexico.

Driver of the Pies
(Sung to the tune of "Leader of the Pack")

They were always putting him down
   (down, down)
He delivered Moon Pies all over town.
   (yes, he drove them all over town)
I don't care about their lies,
'Cause I know that in my eyes
He'll always be my Driver of the Pies.

They said he tried to hijack a load
   (load, load)
That dreadful night he ran off the road.
   (yes he did, he drove it off the road)

But I was there late that night,
When he reached for his last bite.
You're gone forever, Driver of the Pies.

Spoken part:

They say some things are not meant to be,
The Future is not always ours to see.
I watched our dreams turn to ash
When he swerved to miss a '58 Nash.
   My heart lies broken, Driver of the Pies.

He died that night out on the street
   (street, street)
His morning rounds he'd never keep.
   (Oh no, his rounds he would never keep)
Every time I smell a Moon Pie
I can't help but break down and cry.
I'll always love you, Driver of the Pies.

Moon Pies And The Silver Screen

MOON PIES PLAYED crucial roles in three classic Hollywood scenes. As with the songs, however, the originals were later altered. Remember when Mae West turned to W. C. Fields and said, "Is that a pistol in your pocket, or are you just glad to see me?" Fields's first answer was, "Actually it's a melliferous Moon Pie. Why don't we go up to your place and share the ambrosial morsel?"

Movie trivia buffs have long known that originally it was not a black statue of a common bird of prey that Humphrey Bogart (alias Sam Spade) searched for in the script of *The Maltese Falcon*, but rather that of a chocolate Moon Pie in Dashiell Hammett's (you guessed it) *The Maltese Moon Pie*. The change was made after a break on the set one day when Bogie turned to a script writer, who was piddling with his Moon Pie, and said, "You sorry wimp! You eat like a bird!"

And finally, it can now be revealed for the first time that one of history's great movie mysteries originally involved Moon Pies. In the first draft of the screenplay for *Citizen Kane*, Orson Welles's dying words were, "Moon Pie." Since so many people were familiar with the Noble Snack, however, the director decided that more obscure final words were appropriate, thus the enduring "Rosebud."

The Moon Pie
And Television

I N AN OBVIOUS attempt to capitalize on the success and
popularity of Moon Pies, numerous Hollywood producers
presently are considering television programs built around the
Noble Snack. Following are examples of a few:

"Magnum, P.I.E." — An action-packed hour featuring Tom
Sellect as Magnum, a likeable private eye with crumbs in his
moustache, as he chases all over Maui after the elusive evil genius
Wo Fat, who has surreptitiously obtained the free world rights to
the fabled "Pineapple Pie" formula. Special cameo appearance
by Jack "Book 'im, Dan-o" Lord. (Mr. Lord's hair appearing
courtesy of Econo Lube 'N Tune.)

"60 Moon Pies" — A hard-hitting, in-depth probe using
hidden cameras and microphones, on the epicurean habits of
anchors Mike Wallace, Morley Safer, Ed Bradley, and Dan
Rather. One particularly graphic sequence, filmed with a camera
hidden in a Coca-Cola cooler under a pile of frozen Zero Bars,
depicts Morley Safer not only ripping off a Moon Pie wrapper

with his teeth, but then washing down the Noble Snack with Pepto-Bismol. Rounded out by "A Few Minutes with Andy Rooney." (Warning: Parental Guidance Suggested — Some portions may be considered unsuitable for younger viewers.)

"M*O*O*N" — A comedy set in the early fifties depicting the lives and loves of a ragtag bunch of gonzo bakers, whose job it is to repair broken Moon Pies, re-package them, and get them back on the shelves of the Piggly Wiggly and Winn-Dixie stores as soon as possible. Alan Alda produces, directs, writes, stars, films, edits, scores, lights, moves props, does make-up and hair, caters, and serves as ERA advisor in this CBS series.

"The P-Team" — Merriment and mischief abound in this fast-moving adventure series about a crack team of Grenada Island vets who, for a price, travel the world bringing the Noble Snack to the oppressed and Pie-less. Led by George Pieppard, the group gets into one zany scrape after another, only to be pulled out at the last minute by the irascible but loveable "Mr. P." ("I just love it when an Original Marshmallow Sandwich comes together!")

Other programs being considered include: "Family Pies," "One Pie at a Time," "King Street Blues," "Fantasy Pieland," and, of course, the daytime drama "One Pie to Give."

Savoring The Noble Snack

O F COURSE, THE best part of the Moon Pie experience is eating it. No amount of Hollywood or Madison Avenue panache can begin to describe the actual experience. Proper etiquette should be followed at all times for full enjoyment.

Mood and Setting

A Moon Pie may be eaten at any time and under any circumstances, although the most civilized people never serve Pies before 10 A.M. True connoisseurs prefer quiet, dimly-lit settings. In fact, sharing a Moon Pie with a loved one can provide one of life's most tender moments.

Opening the Moon Pie

The package should be opened gently by pulling apart the wrapper at one end, starting in the center with fingers on opposite sides. This method leaves an opening to push out the Moon Pie a little at a time while eating, thus eliminating the need for a finger

bowl afterwards. Also, if the hands are soiled, the wrapper protects the Moon Pie. Always open the package with the label face-out. It is considered extremely bad manners to rip open the wrapper in an uneven, boorish way. People who do so are obviously uncouth and should be avoided in social situations. Immediately after opening, inhale deeply the delicate fragrance, which may be rich chocolate, ripe banana, tempting vanilla, or sweet coconut.

Taking the Bite

Most authorities agree that the Moon Pie is best enjoyed in large bites; the larger the bite, the greater the enjoyment. Falling crumbs should be ignored until the snack is finished, at which time they should be brushed off discreetly at once. Larger crumbs may be eaten.

AH, YES...AN EXCELLENT CHOICE TO ACCOMPANY YOUR MOON PIE, SIR...

The Moon Pie Beverage Guide

Traditionally, Moon Pies are eaten while drinking R.C. Cola (pronounced "ARE-rah Cee Cola"), although drinks such as Coca-Cola, Pepsi-Cola, Nehi Orange drink (sometimes referred to as "Big Orange bellywasher"), and Dr. Pepper are also acceptable. Double Cola is on the approved list but is difficult to locate in some parts of the world. Cheerwine, a cherry-flavored soft drink bottled in and near Salisbury, N.C., and distributed in a small geographical area, also has been approved.

Milk is always appropriate for small children, and all fruit juices are delicious with this snack.

Hot coffee and tea are also excellent beverages to accompany a Moon Pie; the warm liquid is perfect for dissolving the marshmallow and icing on the teeth.

A piña colada is delightful with the banana flavored Moon Pie, although a glass of plain water is recommended for the chaser/cleanser.

A light white wine is excellent during the day. Champagne is refreshing during the evening, especially with the vanilla pies. A robust table rosé or red wine is considered "de rigeur" at dinner parties or semiformal gatherings and may be served with the complete selection of Moon Pies.

Proper Cleansing Technique

At least half of the beverage should be saved for the cleansing procedure. Carefully take a large drink of the beverage and swish the liquid around in your mouth. During the cleansing process, the lips should be closed and loud noises must be avoided. Repeat several times, as necessary.

Leftovers

If part of the snack is to be saved for later, the wrapper should be folded around the remaining part and a rubber band placed around the wrapper to retain the freshness.

Disposing of the Wrapper

When dining in a restaurant, lunchroom, or cafeteria, the wrapper should be pressed flat and gently laid on the table with the words "Moon Pie" facing upwards to inform all passers-by that someone with discriminating taste has dined there.

In other situations, the wrapper should be placed carefully, face up, in a suitable waste receptacle for the above purpose. Wadding up the wrapper is considered "bad form" and can completely negate the effect derived from the actual eating of the Moon Pie. Wrapper rippers and wrapper wadders are no more civilized than burpers and should be avoided if at all possible.

38

Use of the Empty Box

After the dozen Moon Pies have been eaten, fill the empty box with wadded newspapers and seal the lid with cellophane tape. Next, place the box on the rear window ledge of your car, with the long side of the box facing the rear. This is a subtle means of demonstrating your good taste and refinement to the rest of the world. A piece of cellophane tape helps to anchor the box to the window ledge. Putting a brick in the empty box is not recommended; if you slam on brakes or otherwise come to an abrupt stop, the brick could damage your windshield, upholstery, hair style, etc.

Some of the more creative Moon Pie fans have mounted their empty box on springs, so that the box bobs from side to side when the car is in motion. Others have connected their brake lights to a bulb inside the box, so that each time the brakes are applied the box is illuminated. This technique is particularly popular in L.A. (Lower Alabama).

Dining in Restaurants

Many of the finer "family style" restaurants, such as the Po Folks chain based in Nashville, Tennessee, now have Moon Pies available for dessert. (They are often kept next to the cash register for protection.) The waitperson should be requested to bring the Moon Pie to you sealed in its wrapper so that you are assured of the genuine article, not an inferior imitation bearing the impressions of the waitperson's fingerprints.

A truly high class establishment will offer to heat the Moon Pie for about twelve seconds in a microwave oven — just enough to bring out the aroma and to make the marshmallow soft. Of course, the waitperson should bring the unopened Moon Pie to your table for inspection and then correctly open it before your

eyes. After heating, it is served on a dessert plate with a fork to be used for eating.

Should you choose to dine in an establishment which does not offer Moon Pies, it is perfectly permissible to bring your own. (Actually, that's where the term *brown bagging* originated; at first it was known as *chocolate bagging*.) The Moon Pie carrying case, made of crush-proof plastic, is available by special order and holds two regular Pies. The case fits neatly into a breast pocket or a lady's handbag.

At such depraved establishments, you may wish to leave the following enjoinder:

> **TO THE MANAGER: I enjoyed dining in your fine restaurant but was greatly disappointed that you did not offer the genuine Moon Pie for dessert. Therefore, I have downgraded your rating from five stars to four and have sent a complaint to the compilers of the Michelin guides. I would appreciate your correcting this deficiency before my next visit.**
>
> **Respectfully,**
>
> _____

These cards are printed on the finest quality paper in two colors and are available in boxes of one hundred. The address of the Chattanooga Bakery appears on the reverse side. A similar card is available for use in grocery stores when appropriate.

Unacceptable Manners And Uses

THERE ARE CERTAIN uses of the Moon Pie which decorum and good breeding simply do not permit. For example:

• It is absolutely not acceptable to peel apart the cookies and lick the marshmallow filling. This is usually a disastrous effort anyway, for the cookies invariably crumble.

• One should never begin eating a Moon Pie and then walk away leaving the half-eaten pie unattended. This is a direct slap in the face of cultural tradition. Moreover, one should not expect to find the uneaten portion of the Moon Pie upon his or her return.

• Never eat a Moon Pie while singing the National Anthem or while reciting seventeenth century Italian poetry (if any exists).

• Never use a Moon Pie as a book marker. This procedure not only does a gross injustice to the Moon Pie but also usually ruins the book. Although the activities of reading and eating Moon Pies are in themselves pleasurable, the two should never be combined in the above manner.

• It is not proper to offer a friend a Moon Pie which has accidentally fallen to the ground. Instead, dry your eyes and take the soiled Moon Pie home, where in the privacy of your home you can remove the dirt particles one by one and then enjoy the Pie.

• Moon Pies are not suitable for use as earmuffs. Although the appearance is quite chic, the R-factor of the Pies is very low because of their fresh, light consistency.

• Refrain from throwing a Moon Pie even when a friend casually requests, "Hey, toss me that Moon Pie." The only time a Moon Pie should be airborne is during the course of such recreational activities as hang gliding (see *The Moon Pie and Sports*).

• The Moon Pie should not be used as padding under the garments of thin or under-endowed women. If left in the wrapper, it produces funny crinkling sounds at the most inopportune times; if removed from the wrapper, body warmth usually melts the icing and makes for messy clothes (or for kinky activities, which the Chattanooga Bakery does not endorse).

• Moon Pies are inappropriate for use in high-altitude jet planes and in deep-sea research vessels. At high altitudes, loss of cabin pressure will explode the Moon Pie wrapper and spread frosting all over the windshield and instrument panel; at extreme depths, the pressure will flatten the Pie to a fraction of its original size and render it inedible, which inevitably leads to the bends.

• Do not take Moon Pies on African safaris. Natives have been known to go bananas over the Pies, thus threatening to shorten the trip as well as a few limbs.

• Never feed Moon Pies to large dogs. If you run out of Pies before they run out of appetite, serious bodily harm could result.

Special Selections

ALTHOUGH THEY ARE not available through retail outlets, special selections of Moon Pies (by the case) can be arranged through the Moon Pie Cultural Club (World Headquarters in Charlotte, North Carolina). Following are some of the packages available:

THE SENATOR: 8 doz. chocolate
THE DELTA QUEEN: 8 doz. vanilla
THE JUAN VALDEZ: 8 doz. banana
THE WATUSI CHIEFTAIN: 8 doz. coconut
THE EXECUTIVE: 4 doz. vanilla, 2 doz. chocolate, 2 doz. banana
THE AMBASSADOR: 2 doz. chocolate, 2 doz. vanilla, 2 doz. coconut, 2 doz. banana
THE CAPTAIN: 3 doz. chocolate, 3 doz. banana, 1 doz. coconut, 1 doz. vanilla
THE SLAM DUNK: 7 doz. chocolate, 1 doz. vanilla
THE GRAND DRAGON: 7 doz. vanilla, 1 doz. chocolate (last row in rear)
THE WHITEMAN SAMPLER: 4 doz. vanilla, 2 doz. coconut, 2 doz. banana

The Sensuous Woman And Moon Pies

SINCE TIME BEGAN, women have skillfully plied their ways upon men. A coy glance, a brief touch, a shy smile, and a seductive whisper are all tools of the sensuous woman's trade. But the truly sensuous woman has at her disposal a lure so powerful that few men in possession of all their hormones can resist. I speak, of course, of the modern Moon Pie.

Just how, you may ask, can that most glorious of dessert treats be employed to a romantic end? Consider, dear reader, the following ploys:

The Casual Proffering of a Moon Pie

A crowded room, a chance meeting, and an invitation to romance. What sensuous woman doesn't know the feeling of suddenly finding herself in the presence of Mr. Right? Yet how does one create that spark — that special moment of communion? The sensuous woman will casually let a Moon Pie slip unobtrusively from her purse, only to land near or on the feet of her

object of desire. Executed in the proper fashion, this device will prove to be an invaluable addition to the sensuous woman's arsenal.

The Formal Proffering of a Moon Pie

Suppose you are in your favorite restaurant when you spy a man who catches your eye. As your solitary meal progresses, you exchange furtive glances from across the room. He smiles shyly while you burn inside. How does the sensuous woman break the ice? Imagine his delight when the waiter delivers a Moon Pie along with your personal compliments. His love will surely be yours tonight!

The Personal Display of a Single Moon Pie

The more adventurous woman will take an outwardly bolder approach to setting the "Moon Pie trap." For the personal display of a single Moon Pie is often the most powerful bait the sensuous woman can set. A Moon Pie tucked jauntily in the cleavage with the top just protruding from one's evening wear is sure to attract the attention of even the most jaded man. (This acceptable use is not to be confused with the unacceptable use of Moon Pies as padding. See page 44.)

The Sensuous Consumption of a Moon Pie

While many women find it difficult to express their most intimate needs, the sensuous woman can communicate volumes with a single act. Take, for example, the sensuous consumption of a Moon Pie. By following a few basic rules, a woman can elevate the simple act of eating a Moon Pie into a symphony of seduction.

Step 1: As the sensuous woman sits opposite her prey, her first task is to select an appropriate Moon Pie. Color is especially important in this respect, and an attempt should be made to complement both com-

plexion and evening wear. Be sure to select the Pie in an unobtrusive manner.

Do: Slide the Pie discreetly from your purse.

Don't: Line up all flavors and choose in "eeny-meeny-miney-mo" fashion.

Step 2: The next step is to gently open the cellophane wrapper in traditional Moon Pie fashion. Once open, push the Pie slowly from below until just the top is exposed. Now gently blow across the Pie, wafting the enticing aroma toward your intended.

The banana flavor is especially effective if this last strategy is employed.

Do: Gently pull the sides of the cellophane wrapper away from each other.

Don't: Rip the top of the package off with your teeth.

Step 3:   Now, with eyelids lowered and lips slightly parted, bring the Pie slowly to your mouth. Take your first bite, letting the Pie linger for a brief moment before you begin to chew.

Do: Look directly into your intended's eyes.

Don't: Emit groans of ecstasy while casting your gaze wildly about the room.

Step 4:   At this point, in order to maximize the intended effect, you may want to depart from accepted Moon Pie etiquette. That is, instead of washing the remaining morsels away with the appropriate beverage, slowly collect the crumbs from around your lips and teeth with an exaggerated sweep of the tongue. If executed in a precise fashion, this final gesture should seal your fate.

Do: Use your tongue to remove stubborn particles of Moon Pie.

Don't: Wipe your mouth and surrounding facial area with the back of your hand.

THE MOON PIE AS AN ACCESSORY TO LOVE

Many women today tend to overlook the importance of the Moon Pie as an accessory to love. The truly sensuous woman, however, would never consider facing a night of romance without a complete assortment of Moon Pies. Furthermore, the use of the Moon Pie as an accessory to love is limited only by one's imagination. Let's explore, then, some conventional uses of this special aid to romance.

In the Boudoir

Some may consider the Boudoir to be a totally inappropriate setting for something so traditionally wholesome as the Moon Pie. Yet, wholesomeness is the very quality that most American men are looking for in a woman today. One need only to look as far as Julie Andrews or Princess Diana to prove this very point. May I be so bold as to suggest that the sensuous woman should keep a fresh assortment of Moon Pies in her night stand. For those truly special occasions, leave a single Moon Pie on top of the night stand well within arm's reach. In this way you'll be announcing to Mr. Right: "Hey, I'm just as wholesome as Julie." Afterwards, share a Moon Pie instead of lighting a smelly cigarette. Use a large dinner napkin to catch the crumbs.

As a "Morning After" Snack

What could be more romantic than rousing your man with breakfast in bed? Freshly brewed coffee, juice or fruit, and, of course, Moon Pies delivered upon a serving tray will make an indelible impression upon any man. Need I say more?

As a Calling Card

Many a woman has pondered the question of how to make a man remember her after that first mad, passionate encounter. A Moon Pie can be just the solution on those occasions when you find yourself at "his place." The sensuous woman will leave a Moon Pie as a kind of calling card. A favorite trick is to leave a coconut Pie with name and phone number written on the wrapper. Special hiding places are under the pillow, on the seat of his car (passenger side only), and in his underwear drawer.

The Complete Moon Pie Woman

The sensuous woman will employ every trick at her disposal to attract that special man. When Moon Pies are added to that arsenal, the outcome is almost always preordained. No man of taste and breeding could possibly resist a woman who reflects those very attributes. A woman who knows how to entice a man with Moon Pies, how to use the Moon Pie as an accessory to love, and how to employ Moon Pies to keep her man happy forever after is the complete Moon Pie woman!

The Political, Social, And Cultural Impact Of Moon Pies

WHEN THE HISTORY of the world is finally written, there can be little doubt that a major chapter will be devoted to the impact of Moon Pies upon modern man. Even now, scholars continue to study the wide-ranging political, social, and cultural effects which this unpretentious product from Tennessee has had upon civilization. It is the intent of this section to explore two dramatic cases.

1.

Perhaps the best example of how Moon Pies have influenced politics can be seen in the life and career of Southern politician Huey "Kingpie" Short. Born the son of an itinerant encyclopedia salesman from Gulfstream, Alabama, Huey was raised on a steady diet of encyclopedias and Moon Pies. By the time Huey turned thirteen, he had read the *Encyclopaedia Britannica* seven times and, by his own estimate, had consumed 11,284 Moon Pies. Shortly after his fourteenth birthday, he quit school to "spread the good word 'bout Moon Pies and sell them books."

In 1936 Huey retired from the encyclopedia business a wealthy man. At the age of thirty-three he was considered by many to be the most successful salesman in the South.

Upon retiring, Short turned his full attention toward promoting Moon Pies. When World War II broke out, he saw the conflict as an opportunity to introduce Americans from all walks of life to his beloved passion. With this in mind, he attempted to enlist in all three branches of the armed forces but was rejected each time for medical reasons. It seems that long years of carrying suitcases full of encyclopedias had caused one of his arms to grow a full four inches longer than the other. Years later Huey would confide in a friend, "Unconsciously, I suppose I knew that I had become physically unbalanced. Yet my tailor never said a word." Disheartened and depressed, Huey decided to enter politics, having no worthwhile career to pursue.

The Kingpie's climb to national prominence was meteoric. Rising quickly through the local levels of politics, he gained national attention in 1942 by running for the U.S. Senate. His campaign slogan, "A Moon Pie in every lunch bucket," soon became part of the American political lexicon.

As a member of the Senate, Short introduced numerous bills involving Moon Pies. Moon Pie school lunch programs, Moon Pie programs for the aged, and a national Moon Pie Day all became parts of his proposed legislation. Then at the peak of his career, he was suddenly cut down by an assassin. Huey was making a speech on the steps of the Capitol when a young man stepped from the crowd wielding a chocolate Moon Pie. Before the assailant could be subdued, Short had been hit full in the face by the chocolate-encrusted cookie. The press was quick to pounce upon the incident, referring to Short as "that marshmallow politician." Physically unharmed, Short was nevertheless a broken man. His spirit destroyed, he eventually was forced to give up his seat in the Senate and subsequently faded

A MOON PIE IN EVAH LUNCH BUCKET...!!

from the political scene. Ironically, the very product which he worked so hard to promote played a direct role in his downfall.

Today, historians continue the debate over Huey Short's exact place in the annals of American politics. Still, no one can deny the impact he had upon America's conscience. As one historian recently pointed out, "He may not have gotten any legislation passed, but no one will ever forget the Kingpie."

2.

From time to time scientists are afforded the rare opportunity to study a social group or community under laboratory conditions. Such was the case in 1962 when a band of scientists discovered an isolated tribe living on a remote island of the Pago Pago chain. An aerial survey of the island had revealed a large, apparently manmade structure resembling a Moon Pie. Upon actual examination, the structure turned out to be exactly as it first appeared: a forty-foot model of a Moon Pie made entirely of bamboo. Scientists were at first puzzled over this amazing discovery. Then slowly the story of the Cow Cow Hoetek tribe began to unfold.

It seems that one night in 1944 the tribe was awakened by an aircraft circling very low over the island. A short time later they heard a loud explosion and saw a flash of light emanating from the island's south shore.

The next morning the tribe went to investigate the source of the disturbance and discovered the tail of a large plane. In addition, scattered along the beach were hundreds of boxes containing individually wrapped marshmallow confections. At first the natives were interested only in the tail section protruding from the edge of the water. Soon, however, someone opened one of the packages and bit into the contents. Then all hell broke loose. Within minutes tribesmen had gathered up all the boxes on the beach and began to transport them back to their huts. Each tribesman established a cache of his own and soon after this event both the social structure and cultural fabric of the tribe began to change rapidly.

In his ground-breaking work, "The Cow Cow and the Moon Pie," Dr. Eric L. Crotchlow details the rapid transformation of the Hoeteks. In the book's introduction Dr. Crotchlow wrote, "Who could imagine the effect this dandy little Southern treat would have upon an entire people?" The changes were indeed dramatic. Standards and traditions which had survived thousands of years were suddenly discarded overnight. Most notably, the Hoetek barter system was completely rearranged around the Moon Pie.

Traditionally Hoetek men had traded goats for wives. Before the arrival of the Moon Pies, three goats would almost always assure the acquisition of a chieftain's daughter. A week later, however, up to five women at a time were being traded for a single box of Moon Pies. Moreover, as the supply of Moon Pies began to dwindle, the price began to escalate rapidly until a dozen goats and twenty-three women became the going rate for a single Moon Pie. "How extraordinary," Dr. Crotchlow noted, "for anyone to equate goats with Moon Pies."

The rest of the Hoetek story is a sad tale of avarice and dissent. As the supply of Moon Pies continued to dwindle, bloodshed became inevitable. One tribesman, insanely jealous over another's cache, would dispatch his neighbor and eat the booty. The women, on the other hand, having been totally discarded, eventually left the island to find a more meaningful existence. Sometime around 1958 the very last Moon Pie was eaten and shortly thereafter the giant replica was erected by the few remaining men. According to Dr. Crotchlow, the monument was built "in hopes of once again luring that divine hand that had originally dumped its gift upon the Hoetek."

Moon Pies
And Rearing
Children

T HE FOLLOWING article appeared recently in *The International Journal of Child Psychology*. It was written by Dr. Wilhelm M. Clarke and is reprinted by permission.

Moon Pies in the Rearing of Children
and Other Wild Creatures

Moon Pies have an important place in the rearing of children, fitting perfectly into the discipline, motivation, and reward system. Today, child psychologists the world over are discovering the value of Moon Pies as an educational tool.

At a recent conference in Vienna concerning the place of Moon Pies in the education of children, Professor Hemple von Stumpledorf stated: "Vittout zee Moon Pie, zee art of childrent razink is gerstunklin."

Although many scholars disagree over the exact translation of Professor von Stumpledorf's statement, the intent of his proclamation remains clear.

Moon Pies as Positive Reinforcement

Many parents neglect the Moon Pie as a means of positive reinforcement, yet even small children respond without fail to the promise of this irresistible treat. While some experts disagree about the exact age at which children should be introduced to Moon Pies, all readily agree that if the child has teeth, the child is old enough for Moon Pies (and old enough to be weaned).

In a recent experiment conducted at the University of Boogertown, it was clearly demonstrated that monkeys and small rodents learned up to seventy-five percent faster when introduced to a strict regimen of Moon Pie reinforcement. The experiment was set up in the following manner: One group of subjects, the control group, was continually rewarded with unlimited food, mild electrical stimuli to the brain's pleasure zones, and unlimited sex. The Moon Pie group, on the other hand, was simply rewarded with assorted pieces of Moon Pies. At the conclusion of the experiment, the control group remained happy but relatively stupid.

The Moon Pie group, however, demonstrated incredible leaps of intellect. While the mice learned to run the most complex mazes designed by the university's Psychology Department, some of the monkeys eventually learned to communicate with the undergraduates, something the dean of students has never been able to do. In a more recent development, two of the apes have applied for admission at the University of Boogertown and have a good chance of being admitted.

The Withholding of Moon Pies as Punishment

An equally important strategy in the rearing of children is the calculated withholding of Moon Pies in the face of undesirable behavior. Again, parents either neglect or fail to understand the irresistible hold which Moon Pies have over children. A child

raised on a consistent program of Moon Pie reinforcement will quickly demonstrate "acceptable behavior" when suddenly faced with total deprivation. In a case study recently reported in the *Journal of Motivational Learning,* a seventeen-year-old illiterate learned to read and write in seventy-two hours after being given a simple choice: read and write, or no more Moon Pies.

In the University of Boogertown experiment cited above, the results of withdrawal of rewards were both startling and dramatic. When rewards were withheld from the control group, those subjects simply wandered off to fall asleep or collected in small groups to indulge in small talk.

When Moon Pies were withheld from the second group, those

subjects reacted in a much more agitated manner. Among the mice there were random riots and at least one planned demonstration. The monkeys, however, reacted even more violently. Two of the apes regrettably took their own lives while a third sent threatening notes to the president of the university.

Moon Pies and Your Child

While controlled laboratory experiments serve to underscore the effectiveness of Moon Pie conditioning, the average parents simply want to know how they might best employ this legendary confection in the rearing of their children. The basic rule of thumb in Moon Pie conditioning is to use common sense. For example, if you condition your child to expect Moon Pie rewards, do not make the mistake of suddenly running out of the treat. Indeed, small children have been known to become catatonic, while older children often become uncontrollable in such situations. A second mistake which parents sometimes make is to leave their supply of Moon Pies unguarded. More than one startled adult has returned home to find the child sitting on the floor among the remains of what was once a three month's supply of Moon Pies. For this precise reason, a Mr. Charles Furndock of Fort Mill, South Carolina, has recently filed a patent with the U.S. government for a Moon Pie Safe, complete with a combination lock.

Moon Pies and the Progressive Parent

Finally, parents the world over are adopting Moon Pie conditioning as an alternative to traditional forms of behavior modification. To be sure, the effectiveness of a spanking or verbal harangue pales in comparison to the Moon Pie approach. Perhaps Professor von Stumpledorf best summed it up when he told the Vienna conference: "Spare zee Pie und spoil zee childt."

The Moon Pie Diet Guide

A **REGULAR MOON** Pie has only 218 calories, while the Double Decker has only 355 — a small price to pay for such joy. Yet some people have found the pleasure so overwhelming that they have been unable to control themselves. The result often is split seams and broken springs. For those who have overindulged in Moon Pie pleasure, the Moon Pie Diet can be a blessing.

This diet has helped many people get in better physical condition and have fun doing so. Most diet plans are dull as bran flakes and offer nothing to look forward to; the Moon Pie plan, on the contrary, offers an exciting reward two, three, or four times a day. This is the key to its amazing success.

Start the day by getting up thirty-five minutes earlier than usual and taking a walk, or jogging, for one or two miles. If you're really serious about losing weight, you must have the self-discipline to get up early. This is also the only time of the day when you can control your activities without interference. Studies have shown that about seventy-five percent of the persons who start their exercise in the morning will continue after twelve months.

About eighty percent of those who start exercising in the evening have dropped out before twelve months pass.

While walking or running, you can imagine that about twenty feet in front of you is a beautiful young person of the opposite sex, and that you are determined to catch up with that person. Of course, you never do, but this adds some humor and incentive to keep up the pace. (You can substitute a Moon Pie, in your mind, for that person, if this gives you more desire.)

Eat a good breakfast, including juice, and especially a cereal with a high fiber content. For a really different and jazzy breakfast, throw a Moon Pie, cereal, and milk into a blender for several minutes. This is sure to start your day off in a different and exciting manner.

At lunch time, take a walk for at least thirty minutes. Then enjoy a Moon Pie, some fruit, and a low-calorie beverage.

For supper, cut out the obviously fattening foods and then eat exactly one-half of the foods you normally eat. This plan does not disrupt the food preparation for others in the family and lets you eat the things you enjoy.

If you have followed the plan faithfully all day, treat yourself to an evening snack of your favorite Moon Pie. After following the plan for three weeks, you may add a Moon Pie for a mid-morning snack.

* * *

Moon Pies also can help those who need to gain weight (lucky devils!), for it can be the foundation of truly fattening creations such as:

— The Island Delight: a chocolate Pie floating in a bowl of molasses.

— The Honey Bun: a vanilla Pie drowned in a cup of pure honey.

— Eskimo Divinity: two Pies covered by a quart of ice cream.

— Moon Pie Jubilee: This is similar to the famous Cherries Jubilee. Cover a vanilla Moon Pie with vanilla ice cream and cherries. Pour on some brandy and ignite. The results are spectacular. Keep a bucket of water handy in case things get out of control.

— The Kid's Delight: Cover a chocolate Moon Pie with chunky peanut butter. Heat gently in a microwave oven (fifteen seconds).

— The Breakfast Beauty: Cover a vanilla Moon Pie with butter and blackberry jelly.

— Flavorings: After carefully punching a few holes in the top of a Moon Pie with a fork, sprinkle a few drops of food flavoring on top. Some popular flavors include lemon, vanilla (for a double vanilla taste), chocolate-almond, chocolate-orange-cinnamon, crème de menthe, crème de cacao, and rum.

A Testimonial

M S. **MARION HANKINS** recently moved to North Carolina after living most of her life in a culturally deprived part of the country. Her introduction to Moon Pies began when the following note was sent to the author:

> Ron—
>   OK! OK! For the sake of cultural exchange, I'll bite. Here's my $1.55 for the (12) Moon Pies. Do I qualify as a bona fide Southerner, or are there other tests I have to pass first?
>
>   Marion Hankins

Shortly thereafter she was inspired to write the following epistle:

How Moon Pies Changed My LIfe

My friends,
    I am here today to tell you how Moon Pies changed my life. How Mr. Ron Dickson reached down his hand to me, groveling in

my mire of uncultured existence, and gave me a MOON PIE. Now friends, that may not seem like an earth-shattering event, but I want you to know that the Lord works in mysterious ways, and I truly believe that Mr. Dickson's mission that day was to bring me up out of my ignorance and show me the light.

Hear what I'm saying to you!

Before that momentous day, I didn't know even the basics of Southern life. Didn't know "slaw" from "cole slaw." Didn't know from iced tea, country ham, or Luck's beans. Couldn't go into a respectable restaurant without embarrassing myself. Couldn't even speak the language. I said "could" instead of "might could." Didn't realize that "pen" and "pin" are pronounced exactly the same way. I "pressed" keys instead of "mashing" them. I could go on, friends, but hot tears of embarrassment prevent me.

But on that day — that glorious, Moon Pie-in-the-sky day — things changed. I came into the office no wiser than before. I had had a premonition that something was in the air, but I figured that it was just the waste treatment facility over on Tyvola Road. Little did I know!

Then I saw the notice on the board that a shipment of "Moon Pies" had come in fresh from Chattanooga (had to look that up on the map). I've always been one to try anything once, so I shuffled on down to Mr. Dickson's office, plunked down my $1.55, and walked out with a box of Moon Pies, wondering all the while what the big deal was.

Back at my desk I sat down, broke open the box and pulled out a Pie. That tingling sensation in my fingers should have warned me of what was in store. I ripped open the cellophane and the fragrance of corn syrup, flour, sugar, cocoa, partially hydrogenated soybean oil, and artificial flavoring came wafting up into my nose. For fifteen minutes I just sat there, sampling the heavenly odors.

Then I took a bite. Glory be! My eyes bugged out, my nostrils flared, my teeth tingled, my heart fluttered. This! This was what it was all about! The revelation tore the veil from my eyes and I saw! Oh, how sweet the taste of cultural salvation!

Today I speak, eat, and even drive a car like a native Southerner! And everywhere I preach the glories of Moon Pies to the heathens, gaining converts and bearing witness to the goodness of Mr. Dickson, who helped me out of my misery. Why, just this past month I made a pilgrimage to Bayonne, New Jersey, where I lectured on Moon Pies before an assemblage of thousands. And next week I'll be traveling to Cleveland and then on to Waukesha, Michigan, for a midnight Moon Pie rally. I understand that representatives from grocery stores and vending machine suppliers all over the world will be in attendance.

Yes, I've come a long way, baby. I have dropped my old life like a mantle from my shoulders. If any of you out there hear my words and believe — really, really believe — then I want to hear you shout "Hallelujah!" Make noise, brethren, for you have seen the light! Go forth and bear witness likewise, that those with eyes may see, and those with taste buds may taste, and those with money may buy of the fruit of the tree of Chattanooga.

Praise the Pie and pass the R.C. Cola!

The Moon Pie And Sports

MUCH HAS BEEN made in recent years of nutrition and its role in sports. Some marathon runners, for example, claim that the consumption of large quantities of pasta twenty-four hours before a race provides them with an energy reserve when it is most needed. Boxers and football players, on the other hand, have traditionally eaten large amounts of protein while in training. In accordance with this ongoing debate over food and its relationship to physical activity, the following suggestions are offered:

Hang Gliding

A Moon Pie is an excellent snack while "in flight" on a hang glider. The wrapper may be pre-opened and secured with a rubber band for convenience before launching. While aloft, the wrapper may be ripped open with a hand and the teeth, if not previously opened. Note, however, that this is one of the few situations in which wrapper-ripping is acceptable in the rules of etiquette. If the pilot were to use both hands to loosen the wrapper, the glider could get out of control and crash to the ground, thus ruining the

Moon Pie. After eating, the wrapper must be carefully tucked into a pocket and disposed of properly after landing.

An experienced pilot reports that the climactic moment of the day is achieving maximum altitude and then eating a Moon Pie while soaring free like an eagle. This must be the height of ecstasy.

Running

While some runners might prefer eating spaghetti before a race, our research shows that consuming Moon Pies provides the same effect. Moon Pies are also neater than most forms of pasta and may be handed, along with a cup of water, to a passing runner. We do not recommend handing a plate of hot spaghetti to a passing runner.

Motorcycling

The Moon Pie is an excellent snack to enjoy during short trips. Moon Pies may be conveniently stored in saddlebags or a backpack. For longer trips, a sidecar is advisable for maximum Moon Pie storage. We caution the rider to use the opening technique described for hang gliders in order to avoid fatal accidents.

Sailing

The Moon Pie is the perfect dessert to carry on board a sailboat. By using the proper opening and holding technique (see Moon Pie Etiquette), one will protect the opened Moon Pie from sea or spray. If an unopened Moon Pie accidentally falls over the side, it will float for several hours, making it extremely appropriate for survival rations. This may not be true, however, if sharks are nearby.

70

Skiing

Whether you prefer skiing on water or snow, you'll always enjoy a quick Moon Pie break. Some water-skiers like to tuck a single Moon Pie in their bathing suits where it can be easily retrieved. The airtight cellophane package protects the Pie in the event of a fall. Similarly, snow-skiers will often bury a box of Moon Pies in a snow drift halfway down a hill. The Noble Snack is perfect for quick energy. Moon Pies served with hot chocolate also make the perfect *apres* ski snack.

Cycling

The marshmallow from a Moon Pie can be used to make a temporary patch in an inner tube. Try that with a pack of cheese crackers and see how far you get.

Ice Hockey

The frozen chocolate Double Decker Moon Pie makes an excellent hockey puck. The person scoring a goal gets to keep the puck for a snack after the game, if he has any teeth left.

A Pilgrim's Visit To The Bakery

By Fred Wantsmore

MANY PEOPLE GROW up, and indeed sometimes grow old, dreaming of faraway places and cities of splendor. Some long for the fabled ambience of Paris in the spring, while others dream of the bustling sophistication of New York. As for me, I have always been in love with the city of Chattanooga, Tennessee. Without question, no other place on earth could ever provide the allure of this legendary birthplace of the Moon Pie.

And so it came to pass that one fine day I journeyed to that place of childhood dreams. After passing the old train station which is now a museum for the Chattanooga Choo-Choo, I turned on King Street and spied a simple white building about a block away. As I drew near, I was impressed by the sturdy, neat appearance of this building, constructed so long ago. Back then, I mused, there was real pride in using durable materials in a practical design.

Standing in the parking lot across the street, I inhaled deeply, savoring the aroma of baking cookies. Suddenly I realized that I was looking at the site of the creation of the first Moon Pie. A feeling of awe swept over me. Slowly, and with a sense of rising excitement, I walked toward the entrance. On the front of the building only a small, elegant bronze plate marked this site as being the end of my journey. It read: "Chattanooga Bakery." There are no gaudy signs advertising the purpose or heritage of the structure. Undoubtedly, when the Chattanooga Choo-Choo was first placed on exhibit, hordes of tourists swarmed into the Bakery for tours and free samples, thus totally disrupting production. Therefore, nowhere on the exterior of the building do the words "Moon Pie" appear.

Inside, I was greeted warmly and issued a hat bearing the familiar Moon Pie emblem — the tour was about to begin. During the next two hours, I witnessed Moon Pie mixers masterfully kneading the dough; giant cookie cutters carving that famous shape; mammoth marshmallow machines squirting their gooey goodness; and a packaging machine deftly wrapping the freshly baked pies. A conveyor belt carried a seemingly endless line of boxes down to the loading dock for immediate shipment to grocery stores throughout the country. Never could I have imagined such a display of technology and culinary wizardry all rolled into one. To be sure, the entire building is cleverly used for the utmost efficiency.

There are conveyor belts that double back and forth upon themselves. Boxes for pies are stacked neatly in idle corners. Every nook and cranny of the structure is devoted to that single most noble purpose. In the wintertime, even the hot air, fresh from the one-hundred-foot-long oven, is piped directly into the offices where the staff is warmed and tantalized by the delicate aromas.

As my official tour ended, I thought back to my childhood days when I dreamed about someday visiting this wonderful shrine. How many Moon Pies had I eaten since those days? How many R.C. Colas had I downed? The scent of a still-warm Double Decker lingered upon my fingers. Nowhere else in the whole world could anyone enjoy a fresher, more delicious Moon Pie.

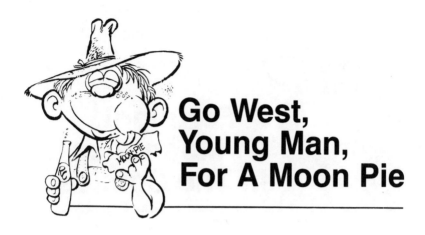

Go West, Young Man, For A Moon Pie

SEVERAL YEARS ago, any Moon Pie connoisseur traveling to the West Coast had to fend for himself. That region of the country was so depraved that few people even knew of Moon Pies.

The mere mention of the Noble Snack would evoke such responses as, "Ohmi*god*! Moon Pies? Barf me out! Isn't that, ya know, like when some dude cruises like, ya know, Sunset Boulevard and sticks his butt out the window of a Mercedes? Sooo grody! Like, to the max!"

Or, "Moon Pie? Yeah, man, I know her. Zappa's daughter."

Or, "Moon Pies? Aren't those the bald guys in bed sheets who sell flowers at the airport?"

In a humanitarian attempt to introduce California to the Age of Enlightenment, the Chattanooga Bakery recently opened a West Coast distribution center. We are all most grateful, like, to the max!

A Fortnight
Of Moon Pies
In The Comics

THE BROAD NATIONAL appeal of Moon Pies was docu-
mented recently when Doug Marlette, award-winning editorial cartoonist for the *Charlotte Observer* and creator of the
syndicated cartoon strip KUDZU, devoted two weeks of his
popular strip to the Noble Snack.

Marlette, who admits that an early draft of *The Great American
Moon Pie Handbook* inspired his series, was duly recognized and
honored by The Moon Pie Cultural Club, world headquarters in
Charlotte, North Carolina. For his contribution to Moon Pie lore,
Marlette was named "Champion of the Moon Pie" (an honor held
by fewer than a dozen living souls) and presented a gourmet
selection of Pies, an official T-shirt, an official cap, and an official
Moon Pie embroidered emblem, suitable for sewing onto his
favorite coat.

Following is the fortnight of Moon Pies as presented in
KUDZU:

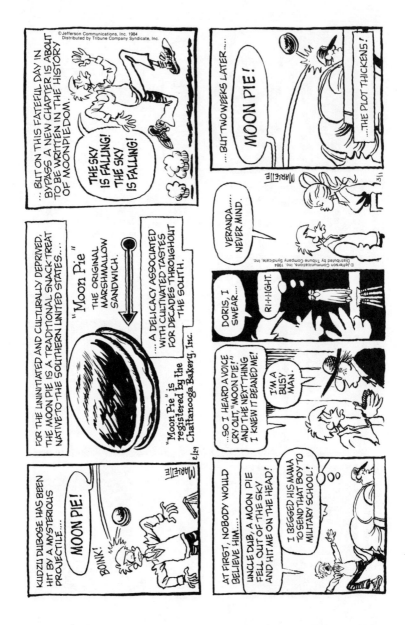

78

WORD SPREAD LIKE WILDFIRE. THE TOWN WAS ABUZZ WITH RUMORS AND SPECULATION... OF COURSE, THERE WERE STILL SOME SKEPTICS....

HOGWASH!

MOON PIE!

ADVICE COLUMNISTS WERE BESIEGED WITH MAIL....

Dear Hysterical, How should I know what to do?! I'm just an advice columnist!

THAT'S RIGHT, OFFICER— IT WAS A MOON PIE, ALL RIGHT....

WHAT DID YOU DO?

I ATE IT, NATURALLY.

THE LOCAL PRESS PICKED UP ON THE STORY....

Bugrass Bugle

MOON PIE ALERT

CITIZEN'S WATCH FORMED

...NOBODY DOUBTED DUB'S WORD AND WHEN A FEW HOURS LATER MRS. MAZEE JACKSON GOT BEANED WALKING OUT OF A CONVENIENCE STORE....

MOON PIE!

LAWSY MERCY!

TO THE LOWEST....

MOON PIE!

WHAT TH-?

WHEN DUB DUBOSE GOT HIT IT MADE BELIEVERS OF MOST FOLKS....

MOON PIE!

BY THIS TIME THE MOON PIE ASSAULT HAD ESCA- LATED ....PEOPLE FROM ALL WALKS OF LIFE WERE HIT— FROM THE HIGHEST....

MOON PIE!

NOW SEE HERE! I'M BIG BUBBA TADSWORTH!

Moon Pies For Holidays, Special Occasions

THE ENJOYMENT OF Moon Pies knows no season, so the delectable snack is perfect for any holiday or occasion. Following are some suggestions you may have overlooked:

January — For New Year's Day, Moon Pies are the perfect accompaniment for black-eyed peas and turnip greens. Peas traditionally represent luck, greens stand for wealth, and Moon Pies are the metaphorical representation of peace and love (the circular shape for unity, the chocolate and marshmallow mixing perfectly for harmony, and, of course, the MOON for lunar cycles of love). Moon Pies also go well with football games and may console football widows.

February — For Valentine's Day, the outer edges of a Moon Pie can be trimmed with a sharp knife to create a perfect heart shape. What more loving gift for that special someone? On Ground Hog's Day, the Moon Pie can be used as bait to lure that little sucker out of his hole. Moon Pies are also welcomed by the throngs of newspaper and television reporters who have been waiting all day for Punxsutawney Phil to show his face.

March/April — The children will remember Easter for years when you treat them to an old-fashioned Easter Moon Pie Hunt. This is certainly a lot easier than fooling around with eggs . . . especially when you step on one several weeks after the hunt.

May — Instead of giving your mother a dozen roses that will wilt in three days, give her a lasting gift of love for Mother's Day — a case of Moon Pies. The long shelf life of Moon Pies will reflect your love well into July, although the odds are that your mom will finish off the case within two weeks. On Memorial Day, it is perfectly appropriate to leave a half-finished Moon Pie at the Tomb of the Unknown Soldier, representing a mission cut short on behalf of all of us. (Note that this is the only exception to leaving an unfinished Moon Pie unattended.)

June — This is one of the peak months for Moon Pies since they are such a perfect treat on picnics. The Pies can be kept cool by storing them at the top of the ice chest. Should your picnic be bothered by flies, it is permissible to take one Moon Pie and place it approximately one hundred yards from your picnic site; every fly within a quarter-mile radius will flock to the Noble Snack, leaving you to enjoy yours without competition.

July — The Fourth of July presents two excellent opportunities to show your good breeding by using Moon Pies. First, when the traditional pig is roasted over the open pit, stuff its mouth with a Moon Pie instead of an apple. Second, Moon Pies make perfect launching pads for explosive rockets instead of just sticking them in the ground. This loss of two Moon Pies is more than offset by the sacrifice you're making for your country's birthday.

August — When the Dog Days hit, turn on the oscillating fan, stretch out in a hammock, and console yourself with Pies. Little

84

chewing is required at these times; the Moon Pies generally will soften and slide down your throat with ease.

September — It's football season again. Time to fill your flask and your Moon Pie carrying case and head for the stands. Although it's not on the officially approved beverage list, bourbon is a very effective chaser for Moon Pies. After several chasers, the Pies will go down so easily you'll think you're in the Dog Days again.

October — Moon Pies obviously are a perfect Halloween treat, but even more fun is dressing your little goblins to look like the Noble Snack. Simply paint two large circles of cardboard chocolate-colored and dress your child in a white sheet. The effect is that of a huge Moon Pie running through the neighborhood.

November — I mean, how much pumpkin pie can anyone eat? Why not treat your family at Thanksgiving and substitute the original Moon Pie? They'll give thanks. For a special treat, put whipped cream and a cherry on top of each Moon Pie.

December — A dozen Moon Pies makes a wonderful gift, indeed, and singles make excellent stocking stuffers. For those who dare to be different, Moon Pies make superb Christmas tree ornaments. It's particularly nice not having to store your ornaments from year to year, since with Moon Pies most are usually eaten before the twelve days are over.

Special Occasions

Weddings — The height of elegance is a wedding cake made of vanilla Moon Pies. In fact, your elegance can be as high as you like, since Moon Pies stack wonderfully. (Note: If the happy

couple has been living together prior to finally getting married, banana or chocolate Moon Pies might be more appropriate.) Send along a couple of dozen Moon Pies for the honeymoon. Some couples fail to come out of their rooms for several days, and Moon Pies are excellent sustenance.

Birth of a Child — Instead of passing out cigars, try passing out Moon Pies. (You never heard of a Non-Moon Pie Section, did you?) If it's a girl, tie a pink ribbon around the Pie; blue ribbons are appropriate for boys. If it's twins, either a Double Decker or two singles tied together with ribbon is suitable.

A Monument To The Unknown Salesman

MOON PIE FANS have been debating for years about the best way to honor the genius who suggested the design of the original Pie. At a recent meeting of the Moon Pie Cultural Club in Chattanooga, the entire agenda was devoted to this momentous issue. Present at the meeting were students, housewives, doctors, engineers, and historians — in short, a true cross section of the American population. The proposal born out of that historic meeting has since come to be known as The Chattanooga Proclamation.

Briefly, the Proclamation states that artists, craftsmen, architects, and school children from around the world "shall be invited to submit designs, drawings, scale models, etc., of a monument depicting the Unknown Salesman and his invention."

Already, designs have begun pouring in from all over the world. Following are a few of the most popular proposals submitted thus far:

The Lookout Mountain Proposal

This proposed carving in stone on the side of Lookout Mountain, not far from Chattanooga, would rival that of the presidents on Mount Rushmore and that of the Civil War heroes on Stone Mountain. The proposed design is for a traveling salesman handing a Moon Pie to a small child. This proposal could be modified to include rows of adults in the background weeping with joy.

The Pooveyville Proposal

Submitted by a swimming pool contractor from Pooveyville, Georgia, this design calls for the construction of a giant concrete shoe. In the designer's words, "The shoe would be approximately forty feet long and twenty feet wide and would symbolize the traveling salesman's most essential piece of equipment. It would be built out of reinforced concrete and have the finest quality plastic liner available to the industry. During the summer months, it could be used for swimming and diving, while in the winter it would be a reflecting pool. As to the type of shoe, I would suggest a saddle shoe, although an oxford or a wing tip would not be beyond reason." The Pooveyville Proposal concludes with the designer's suggestion that "for a nominal fee, I could provide a custom canvas cover shaped like a spat."

The Heidelberg Design

Surprisingly, one of the most interesting designs comes from the Heidelberg Institute of Kinetic Art. Submitted by a group of graduate students, this design calls for a hydraulically operated stainless steel suitcase perched upon a stainless steel pedestal. The suitcase would open to reveal four stainless steel Moon Pies revolving around a blinking light bulb. While the symbolism of the individual components is clear, what is unclear is the actual size of the sculpture. The designers' statement that "it should be very large to convey the significance of the historic event, but small enough not to impede low level aircraft" leaves room for considerable speculation.

The Marcia Mooney Letter

The Moon Pie Cultural Club received the following letter from a Miss Marcia Mooney of Johnson City, Kansas:

Dear Mr. Moon Pie People:
I love Moon Pies. My mother gives them to me every day for dessert. I would like to tell you how the Unknown Salesman statue should be. First you take two hundred Moon Pies and you put them on top of each other for legs. Then you take fifty Moon Pies for arms. Next get the Moon Pie factory to make a special big Moon Pie for the head. Two vanilla Moon Pies could be eyes. This would be the salesman.

Your friend,
Marcia

P.S. Could you please send me one of those special big Moon Pies for a prize?

The New York School of Modern Art Design

From the cultural hub of the United States comes the recommendation that the proposed monument should be in the form of a "plexiglass bowler or derby representing the attire of an early twentieth century salesman. Inside the bowler would be a cube on which would be painted the four basic steps in the preparation of Moon Pies." Unfortunately, several members of the Cultural Club have already objected to this design on the basis that the essence of something as exotically delicious as the Moon Pie cannot be reduced to four simple steps.

The Hinkley, Ohio, Proposal

From Hinkley, Ohio, whose only claim to fame is the return each spring of the buzzards, comes the following suggestion: "It

91

should be, of course, a large granite statue in the tradition of all public monuments. The statue should clearly represent a salesman with one hand extended (as if poised for a handshake) and with a briefcase in the other hand. The only feature that would clearly distinguish this as being the Unknown Salesman is the complete lack of a face." The Cultural Club's initial reaction is that Hinkley should stick with the buzzards.

The Flagstaff Design

The School of Design of the University of Arizona at Flagstaff is among the leaders in new concepts of solar energy, and the Flagstaff Design reflects this specialization. It calls for a huge solar dome made of clear glass or plastic with the Moon Pie logo painted upon it, the overall appearance being that of a Moon Pie wrapper slightly inflated. Inside will be a gigantic Moon Pie carved out of stone with a natural chocolate color. This will be a solar heat collector. On top of the Moon Pie will be a statue of the Unknown Salesman in a standing position, apparently talking to someone. He will hold a Moon Pie gently in his right hand, and his sample case will rest at his feet. The solar heat collected by this memorial will be conducted a short distance to The Home for Retired Traveling Salesmen. It should be noted that this design solves the problem of the passing pigeon. The Flagstaff Design has the twin benefits of being aesthetically attractive and of providing heat to The Home, thus paying for the cost of the monument. Vegetables could also be grown inside the dome.

The University of Melbourne (Australia) Design

This design calls for a large structure in the shape of a Moon Pie box with the lid raised in the display position. The skylights would be stained glass in the shape of Moon Pie wrappers, as seen

from above. Inside there would be a bronze statue of the mythical, Unknown Salesman. Of course, he would be holding a Moon Pie in one hand and a soft drink in the other. The walls of the edifice would be adorned with pictures showing historic events in the story of the Bakery and the Moon Pie. These pictures would be obtained from the Chattanooga Museum of Fine Arts. In the outer walls would be huge stained-glass windows with the following scenes: pictures of all flavors and sizes of Moon Pies; portraits of the founders of the Bakery; and portraits of twelve famous traveling salesmen who first sold Moon Pies to the far ends of the continent. A profusion of live green plants would add to the decor.

The center of the structure would contain a huge sidewalk cafe which would serve all flavors of Moon Pies and a carefully selected list of approved beverages. Thus pilgrims could rest their feet, refresh their bodies, and enjoy the significance of the memorial.

Plans For The Future

AS THE FAME OF Moon Pies continues to spread and distribution moves into the international realm, the Moon Pie Cultural Club is striving to keep pace by implementing a number of innovative ideas. Following are some of the projects included in the Club's five-year plan:

Moon Pie Cassette Tapes

The complete text of The Great American Moon Pie Handbook soon will be available on cassette tapes. These exciting tapes will make excellent gifts for busy executives who need to refresh their minds on the history and culture of the Noble Snack, for the illiterate, and for the blind. The narration will be by a cultured British lady whose accent can be clearly understood by all of the English-speaking world. Background music will be provided by the Vienna Philharmonic Orchestra.

There also will be regional and ethnic versions of the tapes, recorded by famous persons who are eager to add this performance to their lists of major accomplishments. We expect to give some of the ethnic artists complete freedom to express the basic themes of the Handbook in their own words, although we do reserve the right to censor.

Moon Pie Calendars

Two concepts are being explored. One is for a traditional calendar depicting scenes of people enjoying their favorite snack. These would include a couple of scenes from Moon Pie folklore, making the calendar a treasured keepsake for years to come. The second plan would be much more short-lived, since it calls for edible pages. At the end of each month, you would simply remove the chocolate-covered cookie on which the days had been printed and eat it. To insure freshness, this calendar would be issued quarterly.

Anthem

The Official Moon Pie Song will be completed soon and will add a joyous sound to all Moon Pie events. The composer will use a full orchestra to produce the majestic sound appropriate for the theme. A brass section of twelve trumpets and a real cannon would create the proper volume.

A special version will be written for the harmonica, ukulele, or guitar so that the anthem may be played anywhere.

Official Recognition by States

A campaign is underway to have the Moon Pie declared the Official Snack of all states in which it is sold. This will be a fitting tribute to the snack that helped to build a nation, as millions of workers will be glad to testify. The lead state, of course, will be Tennessee.

Poem

A world famous poet, Mr. Vladimir Jones, is researching the history, folklore, traditions, customs, and fantasies of the Moon Pie. His "Ode to a Chattanooga Moon Pie" is expected to surpass even the popularity of the poems by Robert Louis Stevenson.

Moon Pie Rest Stops on Interstate Highways

A campaign is now underway to have the Moon Pie logo attached to some "Rest Stop" signs on interstate highways. This would tell the motoring public, at least those with discriminating taste, that at the next rest stop, Moon Pies are available in the vending machines. The logo, of course, will be small and in good taste, and not at all gaudy.

Gourmet Flavors

An intensive research project has begun to develop some or all of the following flavors of Moon Pies: Peanut Butter (sprinkled with chunks of real peanuts); Cherry; Strawberry; Maple Syrup; Chocolate Chip; Coffee; and Crunch (with puffed rice).

This project involves food scientists, nutritionists, chemists, packaging experts, buyers of ingredients, accountants, our shipping department, marketing consultants, and five small, hungry children who have final approval of new flavors.

MP Cultural Clubs

Plans are almost completed to issue charters to Clubs around the world which are dedicated to spreading the good news. Stationery, membership cards, parchment charters, etc., are being designed. Club members are expected to devote themselves to the cultural enlightenment of their communities and of the farthest corners of the civilized world. Suggested titles for officers and members include "ambassador," "diplomat," and "foreign minister."

The World Headquarters (WHQ) of the Cultural Club is temporarily located in Suite 210.5 of a luxury office building in Charlotte, N.C., while we await construction of our own quarters. The enthusiastic and dedicated staff, entirely voluntary and unpaid, corresponds with Clubs around the world. She also collects, organizes, and files information about the Moon Pie.

A recent project at WHQ was the production of a color slide presentation entitled "The Lore of the Moon Pie." This exciting and humorous show consisted of beautiful color slides and narration recorded in London with background music by the Vienna Philharmonic. The staff is busy translating the slide show into other civilized languages. Copies of this elegant show will be in

great demand for meetings of clubs and civic groups, such as Sierra Clubs, Kiwanis, Lions, Elks, Moose, Ex-Cons, and other groups desirous of improving their knowledge of culture and etiquette.

The Moon Pie Cheerleaders

The MP Cheerleaders are being organized at Cultural Clubs all over the nation. (Our rejects are sent on to the Dallas Cowgirls Cheerleaders squad.) The MP Cheerleaders will be available to add excitement and sparkle to any cultural event (or, in some cases, any uncultural event).

Moonlight Madness Moon Pie Festival

Each year in the autumn, there would be a festival in Chattanooga for true devotees. It would be held after dark in the parking lot in front of the Bakery and would be timed to coincide with the rising of the harvest moon over the Bakery. There would be charter flights of Boeing 747 jets, each with the Moon Pie logo emblazoned on the tail, from major cities in the land to Chattanooga. Overflow traffic and private planes would be diverted to nearby Swan Creek International Airport and Pasture. (Pilots would be advised to buzz the field at least once to scare the cows out of the way.) Toasts and speeches extolling this noble confection would be made by the mayor, governor of Tennessee, and officials of the Bakery. It would be the time for all pilgrims to pay homage and to share the culture and folklore associated with this delicious snack.

The Moon Pie Connoisseurs' Convention

The annual convention would be held in Chattanooga in the spring. The highlight of the meeting would be the banquet at which all past and presently produced flavors of the Moon Pie would be available. All of the gourmet desserts would be prepared by the best chefs in the land.

There would be seminars on a broad range of subjects, such as: "Detecting Counterfeit Moon Pies," "Letter Writing to Get Moon Pies in Your Favorite Stores and Restaurants," "Teaching the Culture of Moon Pies to Immigrants," etc. There would be color films on the etiquette of serving and eating Moon Pies, and shops selling the latest fashions of attire associated with the Moon Pie. For the outdoors types, there would be golf and tennis championships, shuffleboard, and Moon Pie Flying Saucer contests. Each champion would win a year's supply of Moon Pies.

The Moon Pie Patrol

An elite group of men and women soon will be brought together to form the Moon Pie Patrol. These dedicated people will

100

MOON PIE PATROL ...

read newspapers and magazines from all over the world, watching for incorrect references to the Noble Snack (such as hyphenating Moon Pie, or using it lower case to refer to one of the imitators, and so forth). Members of the MP Patrol also monitor radio and television broadcasts for similar infractions. Letters of commendation are sent to those who exercise proper care in referring to Moon Pies; threats of kneecapping or plague are sent to abusers.

Bumper Stickers

A number of phrases are under discussion for use on bumper stickers. Some of the more straightforward suggestions are:

"Moon Pies — A Way of Life"

"Seven Days Without a Moon Pie Makes One Weak"
"Go For It — A Moon Pie!"
Other members of the Cultural Club favor more catchy, suggestive bumper stickers. Among their favorite proposals are:
"I'd Rather Be Eating a Moon Pie"
"Honk if You Crave a Moon Pie"
"Moon Pie Eaters Do It With a Smile on Their Faces"
"Have You Hugged Your Moon Pie Today?"

The Official T-Shirt

The official Moon Pie T-Shirt is, in fact, already available. It comes in light blue with the official logo emblazoned on the front and is sure to cause a flurry of envy wherever you wear it. Refer to the back of this Handbook for price and source.

THE END

Readers are encouraged to send their comments and suggestions to:

The Moon Pie Cultural Club
Suite 210.5
1915 Rexford Road
Charlotte, N.C. 28211

Complaints and unkind remarks will be ignored.

RON DICKSON, a native of Shelby, North Carolina, is a 1955 Magna Cum Laude graduate of Duke University. He has worked as a supply officer in the U. S. Navy, a data processing consultant, and a general contractor. At present, he is facility manager for Burroughs Corporation in Charlotte, North Carolina. He spends his leisure time on his sailboat, which proudly flies the official Moon Pie flag.

SAM C. RAWLS, better known by his professional name of SCRAWLS, is editorial cartoonist for the *Atlanta Constitution*. A native of Clarksdale, Mississippi, Scrawls is president of the Association of American Editorial Cartoonists. His work, which is syndicated by Newspaper Enterprise Association, has appeared in many national publications, including *Time, U.S. News & World Report*, and *Newsweek*. He also was illustrator of the best-selling *How To Speak Southern*. Scrawls lives in Atlanta with his wife Janet and their son, Shelby, and daughter, Lisa.

Add a touch of elegance to your wardrobe with clothing and accessories imprinted with the Moon Pie logo in three colors!

Send orders to: The Noble Snack,
P. O. Box 706, Mt. Gilead, N.C. 27306

SHIP TO: (We ship UPS wherever possible.
Please include a street address for UPS delivery)

NAME

MAILING ADDRESS   APT./ROOM NO.

CITY	ST	ZIP

Qty.	(Circle size and color)	Total
_____	T-Shirt. Adult. S M L XL. Lt. blue or tan. 50-50 poly-cotton. $6.00 each	$_____
_____	T-Shirt. Child. S M L XL. Lt. blue or tan. 50-50 poly-cotton. $4.50 each	$_____
_____	Baseball cap, adjustable. $4.50 each	$_____
_____	Jacket, Adult. S M L XL. Lt. blue. knit cuffs, collar. $30.00 each	$_____
_____	Embroidered emblem $1.50 each (Sew on jackets, etc.)	$_____
_____	Night shirt. Adult. S M L. Lt. blue. 50-50 poly-cotton. $11.00 each	$_____
_____	The Great American MOON PIE Handbook (Paperback) $5.95 each	$_____

Sub-total $_____

Add 3% sales tax if N.C. resident _____

Add Shipping & Handling ($1.50 for
first item and $1.00 for each additional item)

Total $_____

METHOD OF PAYMENT

☐ Check or Money Order
☐ MasterCard ☐ Visa

Exp. Date:

Signature: _____

Add a touch of elegance to your wardrobe with clothing and accessories imprinted with the Moon Pie logo in three colors!

Send orders to: The Noble Snack,
P. O. Box 706, Mt. Gilead, N.C. 27306

SHIP TO: (We ship UPS wherever possible. Please include a street address for UPS delivery)	
NAME	
MAILING ADDRESS	APT./ROOM NO.

CITY	ST	ZIP

Qty.	(Circle size and color)	Total
_____	T-Shirt. Adult. S M L XL. Lt. blue or tan. 50-50 poly-cotton. $6.00 each	$_____
_____	T-Shirt. Child. S M L XL. Lt. blue or tan. 50-50 poly-cotton. $4.50 each	$_____
_____	Baseball cap, adjustable. $4.50 each	$_____
_____	Jacket, Adult. S M L XL. Lt. blue. knit cuffs, collar. $30.00 each	$_____
_____	Embroidered emblem $1.50 each (Sew on jackets, etc.)	$_____
_____	Night shirt. Adult. S M L. Lt. blue. 50-50 poly-cotton. $11.00 each	$_____
_____	The Great American MOON PIE Handbook (Paperback) $5.95 each	$_____
	Sub-total	$_____
	Add 3% sales tax if N.C. resident	_____
	Add Shipping & Handling ($1.50 for first item and $1.00 for each additional item)	
	Total	$_____

METHOD OF PAYMENT

☐ Check or Money Order
☐ MasterCard ☐ Visa

Exp. Date:

Signature: _____